AMERICAN ASSESSMENT

Naquasia Hereford

Fulton Books
Meadville, PA

Published by Fulton Books 2024

ISBN 979-8-88982-431-2 (paperback)
ISBN 979-8-88982-433-6 (digital)

Printed in the United States of America

The casing and boldface appeared as
they are in the original material.

READING AND COMPREHENSION[1]

---

[1] Definitions (lexico.com)

1. "In 1942, a Spanish transatlantic maritime expedition led by Christopher Columbus resulted in the *discovery* of America, a continent which was previously unknown."

    In the above sentence, what does *discovery* mean?

    a. Devising a new use for something
    b. Finding something that had previously existed but had been unknown
    c. Finding or becoming aware of something for the first time
    d. Seizing something
    e. All of the above

2. "Criminal defendants generally have the right to be tried by a jury of their *peers*."

    In the above sentence, what does *peers* mean?

    a. Belonging to the same societal group based on age, grade, or status
    b. Looking keenly or with difficulty at someone or something
    c. A person who is equal to another in abilities, qualifications, and background
    d. A person higher in rank, status, or quality
    e. All of the above

3. Below is a caption from a photo on Usnews.com taken by Getty images of President George Bush during the aftermath of hurricane Katrina.

    "US president George W. Bush looks out the window of Air Force One on August 31, 2005, as he flies over New Orleans, Louisiana, *surveying* the damage left by hurricane Katrina."

What does *surveying* mean in this sentence?

a. Looking carefully and thoroughly at someone or something, especially so as to appraise them
b. Investigating behavior or opinions by questioning a group of people
c. Examining and recording the area and features of an area of land so as to construct a map or plan
d. Watching
e. None of the above

4.

It was during Pontiac's War that Bouquet gained a certain lasting infamy. In a series of letters during the summer of 1763 between Bouquet and his commander, General Jeffery Amherst, the idea was raised of infecting the Indians who had besieged Fort Pitt with smallpox by giving them infected blankets from the fort's smallpox hospital. Amherst wrote to Bouquet, then in Lancaster, on about June 29, 1763: "Could it not be contrived to send the smallpox among those disaffected tribes of Indians? We must on this occasion use every stratagem in our power to reduce them." Bouquet agreed, replying to Amherst on July 13: "I will try to inoculate the Indians by means of blankets that may fall in their hands, taking care however not to get the disease myself." Amherst responded on July 16: "You will do well to try to inoculate the Indians by means of blankets, as well as to try every other method that can serve to extirpate this execrable race."[2]

---

[2] https://military-history.fandom.com/wiki/Henry_Bouquet

The topic in the above passage is an example of what?

    a.   Genocide
    b.   Biological warfare
    c.   Holocaust
    d.   Terrorism
    e.   All of the above

5.   Read the passages, then answer the question below:

> The Atlanta race riot—violent attacks by armed mobs of White Americans against African Americans in Atlanta, Georgia, began on the evening of September 22, 1906,…and lasted through September 24. The events were reported by newspapers around the world, including the French *Le Petit Journal*, which described the "lynchings in the USA" and the "massacre of Negroes in Atlanta," the Scottish *Aberdeen Press & Journal* under the headline "Race Riots in Georgia," and the London *Evening Standard* under the headlines "Anti-Negro Riots" and "Outrages in Georgia." The final death toll of the conflict is unknown and disputed, but officially at least 25 African Americans and two whites died. Unofficial reports ranged from 10–100 black Americans killed during the massacre. According to the Atlanta History Center, some black Americans were hanged from lampposts; others were shot, beaten, or stabbed to death. They were pulled from street cars and attacked on the street; white mobs invaded black neighborhoods, destroying homes and businesses.

The immediate catalyst was newspaper reports of four white women raped in separate incidents, allegedly by African American men.[3]

*****

George Junius Stinney Jr. (October 21, 1929–June 16, 1944), was an African American boy who at the age of 14 was convicted, in a proceeding later vacated as an unfair trial in 2014, of murdering two white girls—Betty June Binnicker, age 11, and Mary Emma Thames, age 7—in his hometown of Alcolu, South Carolina. He was executed by electric chair in June 1944, thus becoming the youngest American with an exact birth date confirmed to be sentenced to death and executed in the 20th century.[4]

*****

Emmett Louis Till (July 25, 1941 – August 28, 1955), was an African American boy who was abducted, tortured, and lynched in Mississippi in 1955 at the age of fourteen, after being accused of offending a white woman, Carolyn Bryant, in her family's grocery store. The brutality of his murder and the acquittal of his killers drew attention to the long history of violent <u>persecution of African Americans</u> in the United States.[5]

*****

---

[3] https://en.wikipedia.org/wiki/1906_Atlanta_race_riot

[4] https://en.wikipedia.org/wiki/George_Stinney

[5] en.wikipedia.org/wiki/Emmett_Till

"Rosewood Massacre"—On January 1, 1923, a massacre was carried out in the small, predominantly black town of Rosewood in central Florida. The massacre was instigated by the rumor that a white woman, Fanny Taylor, had been sexually assaulted by a black man in her home in a nearby community. A group of white men, believing this rapist to be a recently escaped convict named Jesse Hunter who was hiding in Rosewood, assembled to capture this man.[6]

According to the passages, what was the primary cause of the acts of violence in all four instances?

    a. Money
    b. Gold
    c. White female
    d. Racism
    e. All of the above

6. Read the following passage and answer the question that follows:

This speech was said to have been delivered by Willie Lynch on the bank of the James River in the colony of Virginia in 1712. Lynch was a British slave owner in the West Indies. He was invited to the colony of Virginia in 1712 to teach his methods to slave owners there.

---

[6] https://www.blackpast.org/african-american-history/rosewood-massacre-1923/

[beginning of the Willie Lynch Letter]

Greetings,

Gentlemen, I greet you here on the bank of the James River in the year of our Lord one thousand seven hundred and twelve. First, I shall thank you, the gentlemen of the Colony of Virginia, for bringing me here. I am here to help you solve some of your problems with slaves. Your invitation reached me on my modest plantation in the West Indies, where I have experimented with some of the newest, and still the oldest, methods for control of slaves. Ancient Rome would envy us if my program is implemented. As our boat sailed south on the James River, named for our illustrious King, whose version of the Bible we cherish, I saw enough to know that your problem is not unique. While Rome used cords of wood as crosses for standing human bodies along its highways in great numbers, you are here using the tree and the rope on occasions. I caught the whiff of a dead slave hanging from a tree, a couple miles back. You are not only losing valuable stock by hangings, you are having uprisings, slaves are running away, your crops are sometimes left in the fields too long for maximum profit, you suffer occasional fires, your animals are killed.

Gentlemen, you know what your problems are; I do not need to elaborate. I am not here to enumerate your problems, I am here to introduce you to a method of solving them. In my bag here, **I HAVE A FULL PROOF METHOD FOR CONTROLLING YOUR BLACK SLAVES.** I guarantee every one of you that, if installed correctly, **IT WILL CONTROL THE**

SLAVES FOR AT LEAST 300 HUNDRED YEARS. My method is simple. Any member of your family or your overseer can use it. **I HAVE OUTLINED A NUMBER OF DIFFERENCES AMONG THE SLAVES; AND I TAKE THESE DIFFERENCES AND MAKE THEM BIGGER. I USE FEAR, DISTRUST AND ENVY FOR CONTROL PURPOSES**. These methods have worked on my modest plantation in the West Indies, and it will work throughout the South. Take this simple little list of differences and think about them. On top of my list is "AGE," but it's there only because it starts with an "a." The second is "COLOR" or shade. There is **INTELLIGENCE, SIZE, SEX, SIZES OF PLANTATIONS, STATUS** on plantations, **ATTITUDE** of owners, whether the slaves live in the valley, on a hill, East, West, North, South, have fine hair, coarse hair, or is tall or short. Now that you have a list of differences, I shall give you an outline of action, but before that, I shall assure you that **DISTRUST IS STRONGER THAN TRUST AND ENVY STRONGER THAN ADULATION, RESPECT OR ADMIRATION**. The Black slaves after receiving this indoctrination shall carry on and will become self-refueling and self-generating for **HUNDREDS** of years, maybe **THOUSANDS**. Don't forget, you must pitch the **OLD** black male vs. the **YOUNG** black male, and the **YOUNG** black male against the **OLD** black male. You must use the **DARK** skin slaves vs. the **LIGHT** skin slaves, and the **LIGHT** skin slaves vs. the **DARK** skin slaves. You must use the **FEMALE** vs. the **MALE**, and the **MALE** vs. the **FEMALE**. You must also have white servants and overseers [who] distrust all Blacks. But it is **NECESSARY THAT YOUR SLAVES TRUST AND DEPEND ON US. THEY MUST LOVE, RESPECT AND TRUST ONLY US**. Gentlemen, these kits are your keys to control. Use them. Have your wives and children use them, never miss an opportunity. **IF USED INTENSELY FOR ONE YEAR, THE SLAVES THEMSELVES WILL REMAIN PERPETUALLY DISTRUSTFUL**. Thank you gentlemen.[7]

Which sentence best describes the effect this indoctrination is supposed to have on the slaves?

    a.   It will control the slaves for at least three hundred years.

    b.   The black slaves after receiving this indoctrination shall carry on and will become self-refueling and self-generating for *hundreds* of years, maybe *thousands*.

    c.   I use fear, distrust, and envy for control purposes.

    d.   Use them. Have your wives and children use them. Never miss an opportunity. If used intensely for one year, the slaves themselves will remain perpetually distrustful.

    e.   All of the above.

---

[7] https://new.finalcall.com/2009/05/22/willie-lynch-letter-the-making-of-a-slave/

7. Read the letter written by President Abraham Lincoln to Hon. Horace Greeley, then answer the questions below:

Hon. Horace Greeley:

Dear sir,

I have just read yours of the 19th, addressed to myself through the *New York Tribune*. If there be any statements, or assumptions of fact, which I may know to be erroneous, I do not, now and here, controvert them. If there be in it any inferences which I may believe to be falsely drawn, I do not now and here, argue against them. If there be perceptible in it an impatient and dictatorial tone, I waive it in deference to an old friend, whose heart I have always supposed to be right.

As to the policy I "seem to be pursuing" as you say, I have not meant to leave any one in doubt.

I would save the Union. I would save it the shortest way under the Constitution. The sooner the national authority can be restored, the nearer the Union will be "the Union as it was." If there be those who would not save the Union, unless they could at the same time *save* slavery, I do not agree with them. If there be those who would not save the Union unless they could at the same time *destroy* slavery, I do not agree with them. My paramount object in this struggle *is* to save the Union, and is *not* either to save or to destroy slavery. If I could save the Union without freeing *any* slave I would do it, and if I could save it by freeing *all* the slaves I would do it; and if I could save it by freeing some and leaving others alone, I would also do that. What I do about slavery, and the colored race, I do because I believe it helps to save the Union; and what I forbear, I forbear because I do *not* believe it would help to save the Union. I shall do *less* whenever I shall believe what I am doing hurts the cause, and I shall do *more* whenever I shall believe doing more will help the cause. I shall try to correct errors when shown to be errors; and I shall adopt new views so fast as they shall appear to be true views.

I have here stated my purpose according to my view of *official* duty; and I intend no modification of my oft-expressed *personal* wish that all men everywhere could be free.

Yours,
A. Lincoln.[8]

What was President Lincoln's main goal and concern?

    a.   To free all slaves
    b.   To end racism
    c.   To have liberty and justice for all
    d.   To save the Union
    e.   None of the above

8.   Fill in the blank.

Drapetomania—a form of mania supposedly affecting ______________ in the 19th century, manifested by an uncontrollable impulse to wander or run away from their white masters, preventable by regular whipping. The disorder

---

[8] http://www.abrahamlincolnonline.org/lincoln/speeches/greeley.htm

was first identified in a medical report that is often cited as a fanciful case of psychologism.[9]

    a.   Cattle
    b.   Animals
    c.   Slaves
    d.   Children
    e.   Dogs

9.   Read the passage and answer the question that follows:

> "The Nixon campaign in 1968, and the Nixon White House after that, had two enemies: the antiwar left and black people," [John] Ehrlichman told journalist Dan Baum in 1994. "You understand what I'm saying? We knew we couldn't make it illegal to be either against the war or blacks, but by getting the public to associate the hippies with marijuana and blacks with heroin, and then criminalizing both heavily, we could disrupt those communities."[10]

Which crusade is the above statement related to?

    a.   The crack epidemic
    b.   The war on drugs
    c.   The AIDS epidemic
    d.   The stop and frisk policy
    e.   All of the above

---

[9] https://www.oxfordreference.com/view/10.1093/oi/authority.20110803095730308

[10] https://www.vox.com/2016/3/29/11325750/nixon-war-on-drugs

MATH

1. Solve:

POLICEMAN _____ **CIVILIAN**

    a. Greater than
    b. Less than
    c. Equal to
    d. Divided by
    e. None of the above

2. Refer to the scale below to answer the question.

How much more per gram is melanin worth than gold?

Oduno scale—a method to classify the value designated by Baba Tarik A.

a. $3.00
b. $50.00
c. $300.00
d. $58.00
e. None of the above

3. The graph below shows the food stamp demographic for the year 2013.[11] Study the graph, then answer the question below.

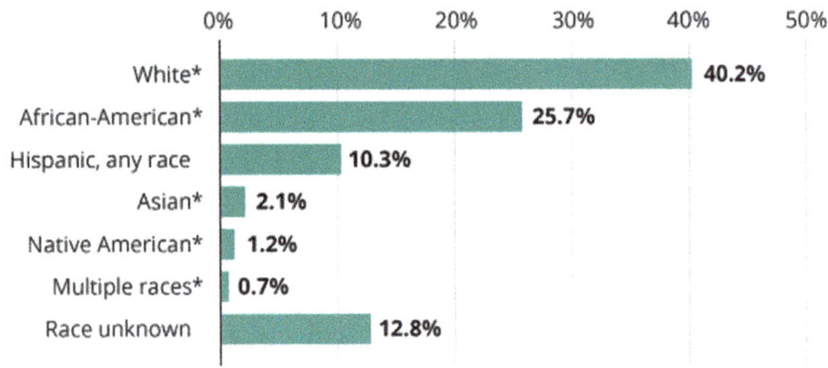

According to the graph, which has the largest percentage of individuals on food stamps?

    a. African American
    b. Hispanic
    c. White
    d. Race unknown
    e. Native American

---

[11] Arthur Delaney and Alissa Scheller, February 28, 2015, 7:30 a.m. EST, updated December 6, 2017, https://www.huffpost.com/entry/food-stamp-demographics_n_6771938.

4. Use the information provided in the passage by <u>Linda Alchin</u> to answer the question below.

> The Three Fifths Compromise, aka the 3/5 compromise, resolved the controversial issue of Apportionment that was raised at the Constitutional Convention that was held between May 25, 1787–September 17, 1787, at the Pennsylvania State House in Philadelphia.
>
> The Three Fifths Compromise was also used to determine what percentage of the nation's direct tax burden the state would have to bear. The Three Fifths Compromise is also referred to as the "federal ratio"—one slave will count for 3/5 of a free man when counting population for seats by state in the house.[12]

When counting the population, how many slaves would it take to equal three free men?

    a. 3
    b. 5
    c. 15
    d. 6
    e. None of the above

5. Read this article by David McCormack for Dailymail.com, published on January 28, 2015 then solve:

> Wife jailed for 20 YEARS for firing warning shots to scare off abusive husband finally walks free—after legal campaign against "unfair" Stand

---

[12] https://www.government-and-constitution.org/us-constitution/three-fifths-compromise.htm

Your Ground law made infamous by George Zimmerman's trial

- Mother-of-three Marissa Alexander was free to walk out of court on Tuesday after receiving two years house arrest as part of a plea deal.
- Her original 2012 sentence had been highlighted as an example of the unfairness of Florida's Stand Your Ground law.
- The original verdict was thrown out after a judge ruled that the court had incorrectly required Alexander to prove she was abused by her husband.
- Applause erupted in the courtroom after Tuesday's verdict and outside Alexander said she and her family could now "move on with our lives."

A Florida woman originally sentenced to 20 years behind bars for firing a warning shot to scare off her abusive husband and two stepsons, has been released from jail to spend the remainder of her two-year sentence on house arrest.

Mother-of-three Marissa Alexander, 34, had claimed self-defense in her original trial and her tough sentence was highlighted a year later as an example of the unfairness of Florida's Stand Your Ground law after George Zimmerman was acquitted of murdering Trayvon Martin in 2013.

On Tuesday, Alexander was sentenced to the 1,095 days she has already served in jail after pleading guilty to three counts of aggravated assault with a deadly weapon as part of a plea agreement for the 2010 shooting.[13]

Marissa will end up serving what percent of her original twenty-year sentence?

    a. 0.4%
    b. 4.0%
    c. 2%
    d. 0%
    e. None of the above

6. Read this snippet from an article titled "Hundreds Turn Their Back on de Blasio at NYPD Officer's Funeral."

> Hundreds of police officers turned their backs on a screen showing New York City Mayor Bill de Blasio as he spoke at the funeral of one of two officers killed last week in what has been called an "assassination."[14]

According to the info given in the article, what was the degree of the turn made by the officers?

    a. 360
    b. 180
    c. 120
    d. 80
    e. None of the above

---

[13] https://www.dailymail.co.uk/news/article-2930214/Wife-jailed-20-YEARS-firing-warning-shots-scare-abusive-husband-finally-walks-free-legal-campaign-against-unfair-Stand-Ground-law-infamous-George-Zimmerman-s-trial.html

[14] https://abcnews.go.com/US/nypd-officers-turn-back-de-blasio-cops-funeral/story?id=27851746

7. Read the article entitled, "16th Street Baptist Church Bombing," then solve:

> The 16th Street Baptist Church bombing was a white supremacist terrorist bombing of the 16th Street Baptist Church in Birmingham, Alabama, on [Sunday,] September 15, 1963. Four members of a local Ku Klux Klan chapter planted 19 sticks of dynamite attached to a timing device beneath the steps located on the east side of the church.
>
> Described by Martin Luther King Jr. as "one of the most vicious and tragic crimes ever perpetrated against humanity," the explosion at the church killed four girls and injured between 14 and 22 other people.
>
> Although the FBI had concluded in 1965 that the 16th Street Baptist Church bombing had been committed by four known Klansmen and segregationists: Thomas Edwin Blanton Jr., Herman Frank Cash, Robert Edward Chambliss, and Bobby Frank Cherry, no prosecutions were conducted until 1977, when Robert Chambliss was tried…and convicted of the first-degree murder of one of the victims, 11-year-old Carol Denise McNair.
>
> As part of a revival of effort by states and the federal government to prosecute cold cases from the civil rights era, the state conducted trials in the early 21st century of Thomas Edwin Blanton Jr. and Bobby Cherry, who were each convicted of four counts of murder and sentenced to life imprisonment in 2001 and 2002, respectively. Future United States Senator Doug Jones successfully prosecuted Blanton and Cherry. Herman

Cash had died in 1994, and was never charged with his alleged involvement in the bombing.[15]

About how long after the attack was Thomas Edwin Blanton Jr. convicted and sentenced?

    a.   4 years
    b.   18 years
    c.   38 years
    d.   14 years
    e.   None of the above

8. Read the article from Qz.com by Annalisa Merelli, a senior reporter, published June 3, 2021 and last updated on July 1, 2021 and answer the question that follows:

> In 1838, Georgetown College—as the university was then known—was struggling under significant debt, alongside other properties owned by the Jesuits. In order to save it, the Jesuits arranged the sale of 272 slaves, including children and even infants, among the hundreds owned by the Catholic clerical order. The sale yielded about $115,000 at the time—equal to about $3 million today—a portion of which went to the university. Some was spent on the construction of a building named after one of the sale's organizers.

About how much profit was made from Georgetown University slave sales in the present day?

    a. $3,185,000
    b. $3,415,000

---

[15] https://en.wikipedia.org/wiki/16th_Street_Baptist_Church_bombing

c. 100%

d. $3,070,000

e. None of the above

9. Read the passage and answer the question that follows:

> The issue of literacy among blacks during the Civil War was a complicated one. Before the 1830s, there were few restrictions on teaching slaves to read and write. After the slave revolt led by Nat Turner in 1831, all slave states, except Maryland, Kentucky, and Tennessee, passed laws against teaching slaves to read and write. For example, in 1831 and 1832, statu[t]es were passed in Virginia prohibiting meetings to teach free blacks to read or write and instituting a fine of $10–$100 for teaching enslaved blacks.[16]

How much could you be fined for teaching free blacks to read or write?

a. $800

b. $85

c. $8

d. $108

e. None of the above

10. Read, then solve:

> In the year 1849, Henry "Box" Brown mailed himself to freedom from Richmond, Virginia, to the Anti-Slavery Office in Philadelphia. The

---

[16] https://americanexperience.si.edu/wp-content/uploads/2014/09/Literacy-as-Freedom.pdf

delivery took 26 hours, and he later became a public speaker and abolitionist.

Suppose the box was 12 inches in width, 12 inches in length, and 24 inches in height. What then would the volume of the box be?

a. 42 cubic inches
b. 48 cubic inches
c. 3,456 cubic inches
d. 5,000 cubic inches
e. None of the above

SOCIAL STUDIES

1. Read about slave patrols in the Southern colonies from a book by Meru El Muad'Dib, then answer the question that follows:

> As Southern colonies developed an agricultural economic system, slave trade became indispensable to keep the economy running. African slaves soon outnumbered whites in some colonies, and the fear of insurrections and riots led to the establishment of organized groups of vigilantes to keep them under control.

The above is the start of which US government organization?

a. Law enforcement
b. IRS
c. Banking system
d. Congress
e. All of the above

2. Fill in the blanks from an article on *Washington's Blog* by Carl Herman, posted on January 16, 2012.

> Dr. Martin Luther King's family and his personal friend and attorney, William F. Pepper, won a civil trial that found _________________ guilty in the wrongful death of Martin Luther King. The 1999 trial was the only trial ever conducted on the assassination of Dr. King.

a. White people
b. James Ray
c. The US government
d. Muslims
e. Not enough information

3. Which crimes are punishable by death in the United States?

  a.   Selling CDs outside of a convenient store (Alton Sterling)
  b.   Driving with a inactive brake light (Philando Castille)
  c.   Selling untaxed cigarettes (Eric Garner)
  d.   Subject of police investigation (Breonna Taylor)
  e.   Not enough information

4. Read the passage from Learn Religions by Catherine Beyer,[17] then answer the questions below:

> The orishas[18] are equated with a variety of Catholic saints. This was a necessity when slave-owners refused to allow slaves to practice African religion. It is understood that the orishas wear many masks in order for people to better understand them. Santeros (Santeria priests) do not believe that the orishas and the saints are identical. The saint is a mask of the orisha, and it does not work the other way around. However, many of their clients are also Catholic, and they understand that such clients better identify with these beings under the guise of their saintly counterparts.

Why was it necessary for the orishas to be synchronized with Catholic saints?

  a.   Because slaves weren't allowed to practice their native African religion

---

[17] https://www.learnreligions.com/who-are-the-orishas-95922
[18] Orishas are any various spirits in West African and especially Yoruban religious belief that can interact directly with human beings, often ritually invoked to influence human affairs or communicate messages from the spirit world (https://www.thefreedictionary.com/Orishas).

b. Because slaves were forced to be Catholic
c. Because saints and orishas are identical
d. Because Catholicism is better than African religion
e. All of the above

5. Below is the history of what symbol?

It is a representation of both physical and eternal life. It is known as the original cross, which is a powerful symbol that was first created by Africans in ancient Egypt.

a. Swastika
b. Ankh
c. Cross
d. Pyramid
e. None of the above

6. Read the passage below that explains how the United States welfare system was created, then answer the questions that follow.

The program was created under the name Aid to Dependent Children (ADC) by the Social Security Act of 1935 as part of the New Deal. It was created as a means tested entitlement which subsidized the income of families where fathers were "deceased, absent, or unable to work." It provided a direct payment of $18 per month for one child, and $12 for a second child. In 1994, the average payment was $420/month.

The federal government required contributions from individual states, and authorized state discretion to determine who received aid and in what amount. ADC was primarily created for white single mothers, who were expected not to work. Black mothers, who had always been in the labor force, were not considered eligible to receive benefits. In 1961, a change in the law permitted states to extend benefits to families where the father was unemployed, a measure which 25 states eventually adopted. The words *families with* were added to the name in 1962, partly due to concern that the program's rules discouraged marriage.[19]

According to the passage, in 1935 when the program started, who was not allowed or considered eligible to receive benefits?

    a.   Families who were married
    b.   Black mothers who had always been in the labor force
    c.   Poor single mothers
    d.   White single mothers who were expected not to work
    e.   All of the above

7. Refer back to the last passage and answer, Whom was the program primarily created for?

    a.   White single mothers
    b.   Black single mothers
    c.   Poor families
    d.   American citizens
    e.   None of the above

8. In terms of the USA, who is responsible for creating proposals for federal laws?

    a.   Legislative branch
    b.   Executive branch
    c.   Judicial branch
    d.   The president
    e.   Not enough information

---

[19] https://en.wikipedia.org/wiki/Aid_to_Families_with_Dependent_Children

9. Read the following propaganda techniques from Wikipedia and
    answer the question that follows:

> *Agenda setting* means the "ability [of the
> news media] to influence the importance placed
> on the topics of the public agenda." If a news
> item is covered frequently and prominently, the
> audience will regard the issue as more important.
>
> *Appeals to authority* cite prominent figures
> to support a position, idea, argument, or course
> of action.
>
> *Appeals to fear* seek to build support by
> instilling anxieties and panic in the general pop-
> ulation, for example, Joseph Goebbels exploited
> Theodore Kaufman's *Germany Must Perish!* to
> claim that the Allies sought the extermination of
> the German people.
>
> *Appeal to prejudice* use loaded or emotive
> terms to attach value or moral goodness to believ-
> ing the proposition.
>
> *Disinformation*—it is the creation or dele-
> tion of information from public records, in the
> purpose of making a false record of an event or
> the actions of a person or organization, includ-
> ing outright forgery of photographs, motion pic-
> tures, broadcasts, and sound recordings as well as
> printed documents.
>
> *Gaslighting* is to use persistent denial, misdi-
> rection, contradiction, and lying to sow seeds of
> doubt in a target individual or group, hoping to
> make them question their own memory, percep-
> tion, sanity, and norms.
>
> *Repetition*—this is the repeating of a certain
> symbol or slogan so that the audience remem-
> bers it. This could be in the form of a jingle or
> an image placed on nearly everything in the pic-

ture/scene. This also includes using subliminal phrases, images, or other content in a piece of propaganda.[20] (Emphasis added)

Which of these organizations utilize these principles or techniques?

a. US public school system
b. US media
c. US judicial system
d. US government
e. None of the above

10. Read about Ruby Bridges then answer.

Ruby Bridges was born in Tylertown, Mississippi, on September 8, 1954. At the age of two, she moved to New Orleans with her parents, Abon and Lucille Bridges, to seek better opportunities for their family.

When Ruby was in kindergarten, she was chosen to take a test to determine if she could attend an all-white school. This was due to the 1954 Supreme Court ruling of *Brown vs. The Board of Education*, which ordered all schools to desegregate. Ruby was one of six students to pass the test and her parents decided to send her to an all-white elementary school to receive a better education.

On November 14, 1960, at the age of six, Ruby became the very first African American child to attend the all-white public William Frantz Elementary School. Ruby and her Mother

---

[20] Accessed January 10, 2022, https://en.wikipedia.org/wiki/Propaganda_techniques.

were escorted by federal marshals to the school. When they arrived, two marshals walked in front of Ruby, and two behind her. This image was captured by Norman Rockwell in his painting *The Problem We All Must Live With*, which is now on display in the White House outside the Oval Office.

Ruby faced blatant racism every day while entering the school. Many parents kept their children at home. People outside the school threw objects, and police set up barricades. She was threatened and even "greeted" by a woman displaying a black doll in a wooden coffin. Only one teacher, Barbara Henry, agreed to teach her. Ruby was the only student in Barbara Henry's class because all the other children had been pulled out by their parents. She was not allowed to go to the cafeteria or outside for recess with the other students. When she needed to use the restroom, she was escorted by a federal marshal. Ruby's family faced discrimination outside of the school as well. However, as the year went on, many families began to send their children back to school and the protests and civil disturbances stopped.

During Ruby's second year at William Frantz Elementary, she no longer needed to be escorted by federal marshals. She walked to school on her own [and] was in a classroom with other students. Ruby had paved the way for other African American children![21]

---

[21] https://www.hilbert.edu/social-justice-activists/ruby-bridges

Why did Ruby Bridges attend an all-white school?

a.   Because her family could afford to
b.   Because schools were no longer segregated
c.   Because she identified as white
d.   Because she wanted to receive a better education
e.   All of the above

SCIENCE

1. Which incident does *not* relate to the definition given below:

   Chemical warfare—the use of chemical agents as a weapon of war and terror

   a. Anthrax-laced letters mailed to federal officials in Washington, DC, and new media offices in multiple locations (Washington, DC; New York City; and others)
   b. Food poisoning in several restaurants in preparation to interfere with the upcoming election (Dallas, Texas)
   c. Nerve gas releases in subway (Tokyo)
   d. Knowingly exposing a community to water contaminated with lead creating a serious danger to public health (Flint, Michigan)
   e. All of the above

2. What are GMOS?

   A GMO, or genetically modified organism, is a plant, animal, microorganism, or other organism whose genetic makeup has been modified in a laboratory using genetic engineering or transgenic technology. This creates combinations of plant, animal, bacterial and virus genes that do not occur in nature or through traditional cross-breeding methods.[22]

   Which is an example of GMO food that can be found in the USA?

   a. Cauliflower
   b. Seedless fruits
   c. Soy beans

---

[22] https://www.nongmoproject.org/gmo-facts/what-is-gmo/

    d.   Potatoes

    e.   All of the above

3.   Read this passage about the pineal gland, then answer the following question.

> The human body is a series of interconnected organs, tissues, vessels, glands, and fluids. Since the oral cavity is used to ingest nutrients and requires consistent cleaning, the mouth acts as a vehicle for toxins to enter the body. Fluoride, found in drinking water and many big brand toothpastes, is one such substance that has numerous negative side effects on the body—including the pineal gland.
>
> The pineal gland is a tiny, pea-sized tissue mass that behaves as part of the body's endocrine system. Although located behind the third ventricle of the brain, some refer to the pineal gland as "the third eye" because it looks similar to the human retina. The pineal gland also connects with the eye through light reception, which is transmitted through the brain and finally processed by the pineal gland itself.
>
> The pineal gland is responsible for secreting the hormone melatonin—the same hormone that contributes to the pigment in your skin and protects you from sun damage. Melatonin has three primary responsibilities, including protecting the body from free radical cell damage, regulating circadian rhythm, and controls the start of puberty in females.
>
> Problems with the pineal gland surface when calcification occurs, typically stemming from poor nutrition, weak immunity, and sodium fluoride. Compared to other soft tissues

in the body, the pineal gland tends to accumulate fluoride easily. Studies show that high fluoride concentration in the pineal gland can reduce melatonin production and lead to disruptions in circadian rhythm—or healthy sleep and wake cycles. Negative symptoms of calcification in the pineal gland are weight gain, obesity, digestive issues, vision loss, mood disorder, poor circulation, and kidney problems. Melatonin deficiencies, possibly linked with high levels of fluoride and consequent calcification of the pineal gland, can lead to premature sexual development, bipolar disorder, Alzheimer's disease, insomnia, and cancer.

Fortunately, however, patients can work to clean out their pineal gland to return its function before serious complications occur. Healthy pineal glands boost nervous system function, hormonal balances, healthy sleep, sharp cognition, and creativity.[23]

Where can fluoride be found?

a.   Toothpaste
b.   Drinking water
c.   White rice
d.   Potatoes
e.   All of the above

4.   What features do all mammals share?

In almost all mammals, the babies develop inside the mother before they are born. This process is called GESTATION. Once born, baby

---

[23] assureasmile.com/water-fluoridation-2/fluoride-pineal-gland/

mammals suckle, or feed, on their mother's milk. Most mammals have hair, and all land mammals have four limbs. However, in whales, the rear limbs have disappeared.[24]

In the case of humans, what type of milk do they feed on?

a. Cow's milk
b. Goat's milk
c. Soy milk
d. Breast milk
e. None of the above

5. Read the following passage from Wikipedia and answer the question that follows:

> On July 17, 2014, at approximately 3:30 p.m., Garner was approached by a plainclothes police officer, Justin D'Amico, in front of a beauty supply store at 202 Bay Street in Tompkinsville, Staten Island. According to bystanders (including a friend of Garner, Ramsey Orta, who recorded the incident on his cell phone) Garner had just broken up a fight, which may have drawn the attention of the police. Officers confronted Garner and accused him of selling "loosies" (single cigarettes without a tax stamp) in violation of New York state law. Garner is heard on the video saying the following:
>
> > Get away [garbled] for what? Every time you see me, you want to mess with me. I'm tired of it. It stops today. Why would you...? Everyone

---

[24] https://www.factmonster.com/dk/encyclopedia/nature/mammals

standing here will tell you I didn't do nothing. I did not sell nothing. Because every time you see me, you want to harass me. You want to stop me [garbled] selling cigarettes. I'm minding my business, officer, I'm minding my business. Please just leave me alone. I told you the last time, please just leave me alone.

When Pantaleo approached Garner from behind and attempted to handcuff him, Garner pulled his arms away, saying, "Don't touch me, please." Pantaleo then placed his arm around Garner's neck and pulled him backward in an attempt to bring him to the ground; in the process, Pantaleo and Garner slammed into a glass window, which did not break. Garner went to his knees and forearms and did not say anything for a few seconds. At that point, three uniformed officers and the two plainclothes officers had surrounded him. After 15 seconds, the video shows Pantaleo removing his arm from around Garner's neck; Pantaleo then used his hands to push Garner's face into the sidewalk while pinning him down. Garner is heard saying "I can't breathe" eleven times while lying face down on the sidewalk.[47] The arrest was supervised by a female African-American NYPD sergeant, Kizzy Adonis, who did not intercede. Adonis was quoted in the original police report as stating, "The perpetrator's condition did not seem serious and he did not appear to get worse."

A police sergeant called an ambulance and indicated that Mr. Garner was having trouble breathing, but reportedly added that he "did not appear to be in great distress." Garner lay motionless, handcuffed, and unresponsive for several minutes before an ambulance arrived, as shown in a second video. After Garner lost consciousness, officers turned him onto his side to ease his breathing. Garner remained lying on the sidewalk for seven minutes. When an ambulance arrived, EMTs checked his pulse but did little else for about two minutes before lifting him onto a stretcher. According to police, Garner had a heart attack while being transported to Richmond University Medical Center. He was pronounced dead at the hospital one hour later.[25]

Which of the following elements would have saved Eric Garner's life?

a. O_2
b. CO_3
c. H_2O
d. NO_2
e. none of the above

6. Read the following passage from Wikipedia and answer the question that follows:

Prior to the Environmental Modification Convention signed in Geneva in 1977, the United States used weather warfare in the Vietnam War. Operation Popeye saw the use of cloud seeding over the Ho Chi Minh trail, [increasing rainfall by an estimated thirty percent during 1967 and 1968]. It was hoped that the increased rainfall

---

[25] https://en.wikipedia.org/wiki/Killing_of_Eric_Garner 1-16-2020

would reduce the rate of infiltration down the trail.[26]

What is *weather warfare?*

   a. The use of weather modification techniques for the purposes of inducing damage or destruction.
   b. The ability to manipulate weather in order to inflict harm
   c. The use of weather as a weapon
   d. The use of weather modification techniques for military purposes
   e. All of the above

7. The following are all said to be properties of what substance?
   - enhances spiritual power
   - the ability to reach higher level of performance
   - targets and destroys free radicals
   - causes younger-looking skin
   - protects against UV light
   - absorber of all energy

   a. Not enough information
   b. Carbon
   c. Water
   d. Hydrogen
   e. Melanin

8. Read the passage by Martha Henriques, then answer the question:

In 1864, nearing the end of the US Civil War, conditions in the Confederate prisoner of war camps were at their worst. There was such overcrowding in some camps that the prisoners,

---

[26] https://en.wikipedia.org/wiki/Weather_warfare

Union Army soldiers from the north, each had the square footage of a grave. Prisoner death rates soared.

For those who survived, the harrowing experiences marked many of them for life. They returned to society with impaired health, worse job prospects, and shorter life expectancy. But the impact of these hardships did not stop with those who experienced it. It also had an effect on the prisoners' children_and grandchildren, which appeared to be passed down the male line of families.

While their sons and grandsons had not suffered the hardships of the PoW camps—and if anything were well provided for through their childhoods—they suffered higher rates of mortality than the wider population. It appeared the PoWs had passed on some element of their trauma to their offspring.[27]

What is the main idea of the findings in this passage?

a.   How events in someone's life can change the way their DNA is expressed and passed down
b.   How the war affected people's lives young and old
c.   How overcrowding in camps stunted the growth and health of prisoners and their descendants
d.   How genetic traits are linked to survival instincts
e.   All of the above

9.   Read the passage, then answer the question:

In October 1919, the *Richmond Times Dispatch* printed what appears to have been a

---

[27] https://www.bbc.com/future/article/20190326-what-is-epigenetics

joke titled, "Game Protection." It reads, "We understand the Florida authorities are going to prohibit the use of live pickaninnies as alligator bait. They say they've got to do something to check the rapid disappearance of the alligator through indigestion."[28]

In the nineteenth and early twentieth century, which of the following was reported to have been fed as bait to alligators by white hunters in the south

    a.   Black babies
    b.   Chicken
    c.   Fish
    d.   Worms
    e.   All of the above

10. Read this article from the Maryland State Archives and answer the question below:

FREEDOM OR BONDAGE— THE JUDICIAL RECORD

The statutes of colonial Maryland established an absolute equation between blackness and slavery. In the words of Maryland's first slave law, passed in 1664, "all Negroes and other slaves already within the Province And all Negroes and other slaves to bee hereafter imported into the Province shall serve Durante Vita." The blackness-equals-slavery precept was reenacted several times thereafter.

---

[28] https://theundefeated.com/features/the-gut-wrenching-history-of-black-babies-and-alligators/

Much is made in historical literature about the legal status of blacks as chattels, indistinguishable from cows and sheep insofar as the law was concerned. But statutory law only reflects how certain people in a society, usually the priviledged [*sic*] class, think things should be in an idea world. Reality often times betrays a great disparity between itself and the way some people would like things to be. So it is with slavery in colonial Maryland. Although the statutes prescribed lifelong servitude and chattel status for blacks, there was also implicit recognition that blacks were human beings and, in some cases, had legal means to freedom. A common-law tradition which recognized these factors evolved.

An example of this ambivalent attitude have been previously cited in law of 1671. Nothing that, "Several of the good people of this Province have to the great displeasure of Almighty God and to the prejudice of the Soules of those poore [*sic*] people (slaves) Neglected to instruct them in the Christian faith." the 1671 law stated that baptism and Christianization of blacks would not be grounds for their manumission.

A cynical interpretation of this law would hold that its real purpose was to attract more slave labor to Maryland by removing a troublesome obstacle, namely the long-held English notion that only non-Christians could be enslaved. No doubt that objective played a part in the law's passage. But, can its clear reference to black slaves as "people" with "Soules" be ignored as mere window dressing? No. Obviously, the whole matter troubled the minds of white Marylanders or the question of Christianizing blacks would have been moot and the law unnecessary. Certainly, the law had the added benefit that Christian slaves could be taught to be dutiful and obedient slaves. Therein lie the implicit assumption that slaves were different from cows and sheep. No Maryland law ever provided for the baptism and Christian instruction of livestock.

It was said that this law would have what benefit?

a. Ensuring that slaves would go to heaven
b. Ensuring slaves would be free of sin
c. Teaching slaves to be dutiful and obedient
d. Teaching slaves about God
e. All of the above

ABOUT THE AUTHOR

Naquasia Hereford was born and raised in Brooklyn, New York, in 1986, and has had a love for writing since she could remember. One of the favorite gifts she's ever received was a blank hard-covered notebook that would allow her to design her own cover and write her own story! She promised herself that one day she'd be a best-selling author.

www.ingramcontent.com/pod-product-compliance
Lightning Source LLC
Chambersburg PA
CBHW040114150726
48005CB00013B/1695